JOE TUCKER

UNITY
WITH
ULTIMATE
REALITY

A special thank you
to my longtime friend
and editor Vickie Nickell.

This book is dedicated
to my wife Nancy
and son Chris
who sought many
of these answers
during their time on Earth.

TABLE OF CONTENTS

1

THE FOUR QUESTIONS
OF HUMAN EXISTENCE

"Unity with ultimate reality" is unity (mankind) with the ultimate reality (God) and God's desire for His universe of perfect order.

Mankind's persistence toward a sense of who we are and the fundamental issues of existence have brought forth a myriad of questions and answers that seek to interpret God's will for the people, planet and the universe.

The vastness of the universe and the intellectual energy of God are incomprehensible to mankind. Through science and physics it has been estimated that mankind may know approximately two percent of God's science and physics of the universe of God's creation. This leaves ninety eight percent of God's nature yet to be discovered.

Within the spectrum of God's evolutionary universal order, God created the planet Earth approximately four billion years ago while creating mankind seventy-five thousand years ago to serve God and His plan toward "unity with ultimate realty."

The disparity between four billion and seventy-five thousand years provides a potential thought that mankind may have been an afterthought of God, as well as, "what is the purpose of mankind from God's perspective"?

Through the source of human reason, mankind searches for the mysteries of physics and science to determine God's desires for the people, planet Earth and the universe.

The first premise of a question is the possible objective conclusion that may reveal the tenets and pathways toward the nature of God's creations. The question posed by evolution: what is God's "ultimate reality for people, planet and universe?"

What knowledge is needed to obtain what God wants us to become? What unity of thought and actions that will provide "unity with ultimate reality?" **The first premise of "unity with ultimate reality" is God is nature and nature is God.**

"Unity with ultimate reality" appears to be evident by the perpetual evolutionary process that mankind has experienced through the ages.

The fundamental issues of mankind's existence have brought forth questions of God's universal order, such as after creating Earth some four billion years ago, what was the purpose of His creating mankind only seventy-five thousand years ago?

Mankind's presence on Earth questions the being and what is the purpose of serving the Creator?

Four basic questions exist to answer some degree of the purpose of human existence on the planet Earth:

A. **Is human existence meaningful or absurd?**

B. **What is the difference between freedom and determinism?**

C. **Does it matter how one lives?**

D. **What is the meaning of death?**

All human existence either past, present and the future share in the answers to these four questions.

All human beings share in these questions through the experience of living. The purpose of this book is to share an opinion toward a unification of thought based upon a narrative of one God, one religion—for God is nature and nature is God. Within the concepts of nature lie the secrets and will of God for the universe, planet Earth and its inhabitants, mankind.

"Unity with ultimate reality" is a change in the paradigm of religion as was DNA to biology, quantum physics and relativity to physics and plate tectonics to geology.

An attempt to answer the four questions of life and its consequence is the theme of this book. If this book does nothing more than raise greater questions and create more answers toward the future existence of mankind it will be sufficient cause for this book.

2

RELIGION'S NATURE OF MANKIND STEMS FROM FEAR

Historical evidence of the cultural progression of mankind finds fear of the elements of nature brought human reason to a state of asking for understanding from a higher order: God. *The seeking of understanding from a higher order was the beginning of what today we call religion.*

The need toward understanding from a higher order was based upon the fear of the elements of nature. The human mind, through human reason, sought to understand the order of nature, but with the extremely limited knowledge of order and properties of nature and God's mathematical cyclical nature a total mystery to the first beginnings of mankind, human reason turned toward a metaphoric order beyond what it was able to understand in regard to nature.

The inability to understand the true religion of God, **nature**, turned human concepts inward toward mankind's self. This began the belief that mankind's intellectual abilities were sufficient to interpret the will and desire of God's plan for mankind. This transposed the religion of God, the mysteries of nature into a man-made form of religion that could be understood and justified in the minds of mankind.

The evolution of religion brought many opinions such as Paganism, Judaism, Zorastrianism, Taoism, Jainism, Buddhism, Christianity, Manicheanism, Islam, Sikhism, Lutheranism, Methodist, Annabaptist, Baptist, Quakers and other opinions of God and His creations.

The manifestation of opinions of God's will and desire has turned religion into an industry of manufactured doctrines of opinionated human design which are metaphors supported by the narratives of assumed scripture. Religions are narratives which create metaphors that become paradigms. A paradigm, through repetitiveness, creates a restrictive consciousness of assumed certainty.

Doctrines of many religions are composed of the dynamics of laws and conversion toward universalization of a culture of faith within a secular order of society.

As mankind looks to God in God's truest form visible to mankind, nature, we find the mysteries of God's creation of all substances and forms throughout the universe.

For mankind to worship God and His creations in the truest form of religion, means to relinquish all the past doctrines and rituals of human design and look to the visible effects of God's creation: nature and the properties of God's creation, nature.

The many doubts of spiritual concern and disillusion can be overcome with an understanding of the magnificence of God's creation of our world and the properties of nature.

The basic tenet of religion of primitive mankind was fear, which with the evolutionary progress of mankind, should be replaced by a tranquil state of universal understanding of God and His will for mankind, which is the harmony of "unity with ultimate reality."

3

GOD'S DETERMINISM LIMITS
MANKIND'S FREE WILL

The centuries of life on earth are subject to mankind by the grace of God and are determinant by God through location and environment.

The location of birth and the surrounding elements of that location provide limited knowledge of only one part of God's world.

Mankind's knowledge is incapable of knowing the spectrum of thought of the total world as God sees and knows. Consequently, mankind is subject to God's determinism by his location and environment. The location provides certain environmental aspects that become the knowledge and experience of that location.

Mankind's free will is subject to both location and environment for the knowledge and experience received are limited to the scope of reality presented by the location and environment.

The Eskimo of the far north has no idea of the human needs of the tribes in Africa toward maintaining a daily life of continued existence, as do the tribes in Africa know little of the Eskimo's daily needs. Both are subject to different locations and environments that present limitations of free will within God's determinism of location and environment. To exemplify God's determinism, which is the evolutionary process, God sets the Thanksgiving table with turkey, ham, oyster dressing, plain dressing, pumpkin and mince pie. Mankind chooses by free will each of the desires he or she wants but the table that created the free choices of man was the determinism of universal causality toward God's desire of "unity with ultimate reality." Therefore, mankind's free will is subject to the knowledge of the table set by God in regard to location and environment.

The Grand Table of determinism set before mankind are God's laws of order and mathematical cyclical nature. These laws are the laws of cause and effect that create the evolutionary progress toward "unity with ultimate reality."

The universe is governed by strict deterministic physical laws, which provide no change, no randomness. Each event is a causal physical necessity of which there is no appeal. God's laws of cyclical nature are constant and consistent. Any object that has mathematical predictability does not have free will.

Within the spectrum of God's creations mankind's existence on Earth is deterministic. Therefore, mankind is subject to determinism and is limited in free will by location and environment which incorporates the sensatory abilities of the human body and mind—which are all subject to the factors of God's determinism—which mankind calls genetics.

The maintenance of body and mind of the human being

requires needs that consume time and effort to maintain. Hunger, shelter, apparel and daily maintenance require time spent toward acquisition, which is a decided determinism toward time spent to acquire. Free will lies within the strict realm of acquisition.

The evolution of human life on planet earth has been a product of human reason determined by the many needs of human existence and the emotions and passions of purpose toward an objective of God's creation of "unity with ultimate reality."

Early mankind's fear of the elements of weather, predators, plus his needs of warmth and shelter, brought an understanding in the minds of mankind for a higher authority to exist, which possibly could provide answers and protection from that which was not understood.

The attempt to understand the unknowns within the world has brought an array of concepts produced by human reason, which has been subjected to location and environment of the authors.

Philosophy and theology of the past has produced many concepts of human existence such as Plato's concept of life as seeing images on a cave wall brought about by a fire outside the cave with images moving past the fire. Homer's description of what brought fear into the hearts of mankind was that which brought about religion. Judaism's concept of sacrifices of living toward acquiring God's favor. The story of God's favoritism toward what was thought "God's special people" which then led to a land already inhabited by the Canaanites. These are the centuries of belief of authors of the past that were subject to the limited intellect of their location and environment.

The past history of religion has created doctrines through limited intellect determined by location and environment, such as Jesus' creation of a perception of an apocalyptic time span between good and evil.

The state of chaos within the creation of God's universe is a source of God's oppression, creating a will to passion.

The beginnings of a church based upon the limited concepts of the emotions and passions were obtained in a limited location and environment. This included looking within the reflection of mankind rather than looking through the reflection of God through space, time and matter provided by God through the realm of nature.

Scripture reflects the human concept for the value of scripture is to recognize the theological claims about God that are really anthropological claims about ourselves.

Because of the lack of substance of the theology available to mankind, the ego of many brought about a reformation to an already deficient concept of God's purpose for His world and mankind. The reformation brought about a more intense facility of discontentment and confusion, which continues throughout the world today.

Mankind insists upon putting a face on God through a vision of self worth, which is pure egotism.

God, the Creator of the universe, is the intellectual energy which no human mind is capable of conceiving. To think any human mind could create or conceive of the mathematical cyclical nature of the universe is contrary to the human limits of determinism of location and environment.

Through the centuries of life on earth mankind has believed certain individuals had certain acquiesce with God, such as the Aryans who invaded the Indus Valley, Abraham and his Jewish nation with Moses' leadership that invaded and took over the Canaan Empire and its people, Jesus and the age of apocalypticism, Muhammad, who from 610 A.D. to 632 A.D. received the words of the Qur'an to establish Islam. Later came the reformation with Luther, Zwingli, Calvin and today the largest religious sect in America is the Baptist Church, which was established in 1639 by Roger Williams.

Through the ages of mankind's existence on earth, mankind has relegated God to the image of mankind. This is the greatest falsity of the human conception of God, the Creator of all existence, which is the manifestation of the mathematical cycle of nature. The mathematical cycle of nature is the evolutionary process that pervades the universe each and every moment of time, as time is the quantifier of mankind's generational process while God is outside of time, eternal.

Mankind's generational concepts of God's providence have created many irrational and irrelevant concepts and perceptions of God's intent and will for mankind.

The multitude of religion's doctrines are based on the self reflection of mankind's chaotic concern with himself through salvation, as in contrast of continued existence, which exemplifies mankind's propensity toward self worth over commitment to the trust of God and God's plan.

God's plan of mathematical cyclical nature is a plan of

progressive evolutionary order while mankind provides chaos to the order of the plan. This stems from the limited free will given to mankind by God through human reason and the divine nature that God created within mankind toward virtue.

Mankind today, through its myriad of religious doctrines and deities is quintessentially experiencing spiritual poverty. The confusion and frustration has been brought about by an industry of religion, which provides consistent controversy on who is right with their interpretation of God and God's will.

The purpose of this book is to unify God's purpose for the universe and mankind toward 'unity with ultimate reality.'

The truest form of God's will for mankind and the recognition of the purist form of God's intent for mankind will be a religion based upon "the order of nature" which is the only visible form of God known to mankind.

A religion based upon the order of nature will hold in contempt murder of any of God's creations, incest, rape, hate, anger and foremost the intent to use and dominate mankind for the purpose of power and profit.

A religion based upon "the order of nature" would focus on the distribution of basic human needs throughout the world rather than the present concept to allow human needs subject to barter and profit, which has created conflict and destruction throughout the world.

Within certain societies and countries, the word "capitalism" means less freedom for the populace. This concept is the essence of power and profit by allowing basic human services to be bartered, therefore, limited to a certain few which creates confusion, frustration, hate and consequently conflict between those of power and profit and those of poverty.

Within America and what is termed "the free world", the concept of nation building through the profit motive is the prevalent idea of success.

The doctrine of capitalism is thought to be the motive of success through profit, which in turn begets power. The current motives of success of capitalism are contrary to capitalism's author, Adam Smith, whose motive of success of capitalism was based upon sympathy and empathy. A capitalism of sympathy and empathy provides a harmonious social structure of distribution of human needs, which creates far more freedom of human thought than the restrictions of poverty.

A culture of harmony provides far more freedom than a culture of profit and power. For those of profit and power feel greater freedom but at a cost to others who are less fortunate and restricted to less freedom. This means the harmony of society is restricted from the full potential of society limited toward the evolutionary process God desires of "unity with ultimate reality."

Currently the concept of nation building with the capitalism doctrine of profit has little appeal to many Muslim nations, whereas a concept of capitalism with sympathy and empathy may find an acceptance not yet experienced.

4

THE VALUE OF SCRIPTURE IS ANTHROPOLOGICAL CLAIMS ABOUT OURSELVES

Metaphor, language and narrative are the tools of human existence. Religions are metaphors supported by scripture that is limited by location and environment. To recognize the reality of religion, one must recognize religion is composed of both history and myth. In many cases history has been built upon myth.

The history of religion is based upon the "oracle" which is a story told, often repeatedly, then later written down. An "oracle" is often influenced by several opinions.

Conceptually, religion's narratives are compositions of myth, metaphor and history, composed and authored by mankind. Everyday reality is history, but myth lies beyond history and to recognize the difference between myth and history is of paramount importance to discover the truth.

Religion has been subject to its history being built on myth through the referencing of oracles to develop the author's narratives. Religion's narratives have become metaphors, that through repetitiveness, have become *paradigms of consciousness of assumed certainty.*

Religion's narratives have been throughout history, subject to the human ego's of the first church and its founding elders, as well as the reformation and the many ego's that have formed religion's house of art and thought. The value of scripture is to recognize the theological claims about God are really anthropological claims about ourselves.

The very beginnings of man's religious concepts came from fear. Fear of nature's culmination of powers, some benevolent and some hostile, such as water and fire, sun and rain, day and night. Since all these factors of life were beyond man's control, consequently, man subjected his fear to a higher power. God's power of nature's laws and purposes brought man into a belief of a greater authority, whereby the people of the ancient world thought their gods were of the world of nature.

Later in history an Egyptian goddess, Hathor, brought to light the fertility of a woman is consistent with the agricultural year, in there is a period of fallowness, followed by a period of fertility, and then a harvest, followed by another period of fallowness.

Procreation is subject to women's menstrual cycle and with the agricultural cycle the same as the women's menstrual, does this not prove woman is of this earth and man emanates from woman? Therefore, both men and women are of this earth.

The generational process of God's earth is the growth of organic matter which depends upon the death of other organic matter. This is evidenced by the birth of planet earth by the death of another star. Birth and death are laws of nature that bring forth new evolutionary development toward God's plan of "unity with ultimate reality".

God created space, time and matter. Man's destiny on this earth and possibly the universe is to form matter for further generations so they too can further the evolutionary process of "unity with ultimate reality".

"Unity with ultimate reality" is man with God's ultimate purpose for the universe, earth and man. God's ultimate world conceptually is far beyond today's human mind to comprehend, for God did not create the world for one generation of man but for many generations of mankind to improve and bring the world and universe into a state of perpetual purity of both soul and soil. The quest for purification of soul and soil is God's divine will for mankind before sleeping with his ancestors.

Mankind's assumption that polluting the earth and diminishing its resources is the prerogative of mankind is contrary to the purpose God created man for. Many generations have come from poverty of thought and consumption and are not aware of maintaining lifestyles of conservative purity of both soul and soil.

5

THE VIRTUE OF HUMAN REASON IS OFTEN IN CONFLICT WITH THE HUMAN BODY

Human reason is the divine nature God created within man toward virtue.

Mankind's body is made from this earth and when it dies it returns to earth.

Human reason, the God given ability to think and reason, was given by God to only one animal on earth, man.

The body and the gift of human reason are in substantial conflict, which creates both oppression and repression within the individual, which frequently creates passion.

The accommodation of the soul to the secular demand of what is considered acceptable to society often creates added repression to the oppressed commitment to the service of God's purpose for mankind to serve his destiny for Him.

The one real religion is God's nature and his laws, for they cannot be commanded but obeyed. The true symbol of God's religion, nature, is the circle, which indicates recurrence and perpetuality.

When considering God's process of evolution, human existence is based upon generation, whereas anything that becomes greater must become greater after being less. This is demonstrated throughout the universe by the death of planets and stars that convert energy into other matter which become bodies of the universe. This is the evolutionary process of God's plan for this world and universe. This explains God's reason for death.

While mankind endures change, God's will is change, which is the evolutionary process toward "unity with ultimate reality", through change, which to understand God's plan for the world and mankind that inhabits it, we must understand God's composition of mankind.

Foremost, God's creation of man is of God Himself, not in human likeness but within the intellectual energy man calls God. **Human reason is the divine nature God has created within man toward virtue.**

Human reason, the gift of God, lives in a body of this earth. The body of this earth is composed of a myriad of sensations and impulses. Human reason is then dependent upon the body for external input since knowledge has its origin from external perception. Reason is then dependent upon the body for external input since knowledge has its origin from external perception.

The conflict between matter that is the composition of this planet which contains all the prerequisites of existence is in contrast to the divine nature of human reason. This conflict and contrast is the divine nature of God's gift of human reason and the body's myriad of sensations provided by external perceptions.

The body, composed of all the earth bound elements, has definitive needs to maintain existence. The needs of the body are breath, food, shelter and natural selection through companionship, all of which are immediate and constant.

When the earth bound body's needs are not met, fear of survival becomes a primary concern of the divine nature God has created with man, human reason. The body's will to live is imposed upon the divine nature God has created within man, human reason, creating the con-flict of heaven (soul) and earth (sensations), therefore, it must be concluded that sin and transgressions are of this earth.

6

MANKIND'S PURPOSE ON EARTH IS TO FORM MATTER INTO FUNCTION

The fear and transgressions origined of this earth have been the source of most religions and doctrines that are recognized in today's societies.

Fear is not a good foundation in which to build. Secular societies have throughout history used fear for control of societies. This has placed most religions conceptually into a state of moral laws such as Judaism, Christianity and Islam. The laws of moral order attempt to prohibit greed, power, killing, wealth, possession and materialism, all created by the sensations the body needs against fear of non-existence.

To realize our bodies are of this earth and the earth is a source of fear is to recognize the true nature and religious doctrine of God's will for human existence on planet earth.

The earth is of the matter created by God that is of sinful nature. Consequently, since the human being is a composition of earth, the body of man is of the sinful sensations of earth.

Human reason is the divine nature God created within man toward virtue. Consequently, all is not perfect in God's world for the conflict between matter, (which is the composition of the planet), also contains all of the prerequisites of existence which are often in contrast to the divine nature of human reason.

God's will for man is to overcome the fear of collection, such as greed, power, killing, possession, wealth, materialism and to rely on the divine nature of virtue, which provides through knowledge "unity with ultimate reality".

The evolutionary process of nature is the divine nature of God. Human reason is to overcome and transpose the earth's elements of sin into elements of reason and goodness. This is the purification process of God's "unity with ultimate reality".

Mankind today believes the paramount importance of man is greater than the planet earth. We must remember God created earth long before He created man. While the planet lives on for many generations, mankind only occupies a limited time and space before their bodies return to earth from which they came. This means the earth reclaims all its sins and sensations that were once manifested in the body of man.

The soul, the divine nature of virtue, which is only on loan to the body while on earth, returns to its owner, God. This is the true salvation of mankind.

Today, religion has created a superior connotation that man is of greater worth than the planet in which we live. This is an ego trip of personal self worth, for mankind is the tool of God to shape matter toward the evolutionary process of "unity with ultimate reality".

God's secrets through discovery through human reason

are the way toward the next generations' better life, for m
ankind is assigned by God upon the time of his creation to
serve God in man's finite time toward God's plan for this
planet and universe toward the future, "unity with ultimate
reality".

7

**MANKIND'S NEED
TO KNOW GOD**

God's will is not conflict, but "unity with ultimate reality," meaning mankind with God and God's purpose. This will bring to man the consonant way of living in God's world.

Nature is the will and commands of God toward the future of this world and the universe. No other religious doctrine or deities should stand in front of God and the nature He created.

The many faces of God created by man, and the scriptures written by man out of an age of persecution are the manufactured assumptions created by man from fear. Fear of future need, fear creating greed, fear creating want of greater wealth, fear of lack of power, fear creating greater ego and importance, fear of being alone and overburdened with life's oppression and repression. The many faces of fear, which began the first concepts toward God, gods and goddesses in man's early history, are today carried on as the face of religions.

The world's religions to date are all built upon human assumptions of the past which have incorporated the fears of mankind. This, in turn, has created religions of laws that have in turn created further persecution and fear which has allowed history to show that many religions have inspired battles, beginning with the Aslayans in the Indus Valley to today's conflict between Israel and Palestine.

The consonant way of life on earth is not to pollute but to purify. To bring the earth, which is the composition of our earth bound bodies, in tune with a purified human reason that is the creative nature of God toward virtue.

God's will in the future will no longer be determined by assumptions created by persecution, stress, greed, power, fear and wealth, and be prevalent over virtue. Virtue will provide understanding that fear has no place for mankind to dwell; that looking toward nature and it's hidden promises of the future, man can find God's desires toward his ultimate world.

God created mankind to be happy and productive. Fear and stress are counterproductive to God's expectations of man. War and poverty are delineations of mankind's progress toward "unity with ultimate reality".

Wars are symptoms of power which creates greater power. War begets war; power begets power, both of which are man made regressions toward the objective of God's will for this world and universe.

Born with God's creative virtue, known as human reason, with a body of this world of sensations and needs, the newborn comes into a world of uncertainty and anxiety with a need for an infallible source of knowledge that provides seemingly some assured answers for questions we often do not know. This is often seen in children who are assured they do not know, but their parents do. This exemplifies our need for an all-knowing father, God.

8

OPPOSITION IS A TOOL
TOWARD TRUTH

Within God's universe, opposition appears to be the concept of the "will to power." Power comes from electricity because of positive and negative poles. The moon creates a gravitational pull that creates the tides. Mankind searches for truth and goodness through the opposition of falsity and evil.

The composition of mankind's body is of this earth, which creates emotions of necessity of existence, which appear to be both good and bad. Mankind's strength of character is determined by the power of human reason's virtue over the body's emotions of necessity of existence.

Since the body of mankind is in contrast to the virtue of human reason, a certain conclusion could be assumed; **the earth is of certain negative opposition to mankind's human reason of a virtuous nature**. Within this concept, the power of opposition created by God may define more accurately the definition of good and evil.

The rhythm of nature appears to gain its power from opposition, such as birth from death, matter to energy and then energy to matter or heat. God's creation of opposition within the universe is a source of power created out of contention toward conversion toward the good of "unity with ultimate reality."

The opposition of time and space is the nature of change; change from the past to the present and from the present to the future. Opposition is nature's evolutionary rhythm toward purification of the universe toward "unity with ultimate reality." The hope of the future is the opposition created by God throughout the universe which purifies the universe toward "unity with ultimate reality."

Human existence is a part of nature's rhythm in the universe.

For mankind to obtain "unity with ultimate reality," mankind must see the beauty of nature, the rhythm of the universe, which includes God's creation of oppositional forces creating the power and energy throughout the universe.

God's mathematical cynical nature of opposition includes plus and minus, good and bad, divine and evil, up and down, right and left, gravitation and vacuum, life and death, forward and backward. Within the life span of matter the tension of opposition within the universe creates and destroys as the conversion of nature's rhythm alters time and space.

God's creation of opposition is both the knowledge of the known and the unknown to mankind. The controversy of the unknown today becomes the known of tomorrow.

Mankind's future within God's universe is the introspection of opposition toward the divine nature of God and God's mathematical cyclical nature toward "unity with ultimate reality." For mankind to arrive to an understanding of "unity with ultimate reality", mankind will have to gain the knowledge of righteousness from the universe of opposition.

Mankind, in today's world, is in a state of regression through indifference created by greed, profit, wealth, power and the basic will to oppress for self benefit, for oppression creates opposition and the human factor of opposition has greatly increased with the new age of greater communication.

Tomorrow's religion of the world will recognize the oppressions of conversion and pursue the righteousness from God's creation of opposition as an energy source toward "unity with ultimate reality." The pursuit of God's truth is the highest order toward mankind's destiny toward "unity with ultimate reality."

The pursuit of righteous truth of God's mathematical universal cyclical nature lessens the oppositional forces, which in turn lessens the oppression on mankind.

The conflict of religion today is the continued and concerted practice of preaching indifference, which has created greater opposition and increased fractionalization of the world's religions.

9

EVOLUTION WILL CHANGE
THE SENSE OF RELIGION

In the past, mankind has created mythical figures of earth bound nature to provide both a social and personal security of mind toward a seemingly untroubled faith toward ultimate wisdom.

The religions of the world have been based upon and promoted as religions of moral laws set down by men who have been assumed more acquiescent of God's wishes than most. These persons represent a standard as a father figure as does a child to his father.

The religions of moral laws and accountability have served relatively well in the evolutionary process of mankind from gods and goddesses to one God.

Religion today will not be the religion of tomorrow, for increased knowledge will challenge the mythical figures and literature of the past. From this challenge will come new, refined concepts of God's wishes for mankind.

As the world grows smaller through the speed of communication and transportation, mankind will find a need for commonality toward earthly needs and desires. Through proper distribution toward the world's needs and desires, war and killing of mankind will find it's not God's wish to destroy His creations. When mankind fulfills God's wishes toward "unity with ultimate reality", power and wealth will not mean luxury above the norm, but the ability to distribute the needs and desires throughout the populace.

Those who use power and wealth for the masses while remaining humble toward God's "unity with ultimate reality" will become the prophets of the future. A passion of power through humility is the virtuous nature of God.

While the prophets and scripture of the past were primarily born out of persecution, (Old Testament between 800 BC to 400 BC and New Testament 15 AD to about 215 AD) the evolution of religion will be aimed toward relief of oppression and repression that will allow the human mind less uncertainty and anxiety toward fulfilling the needs of everyday life. The world's needs and desires will ultimately be fulfilled by science and technology through the laws of nature which are of God's creation.

God's laws of nature are profound and lie within secrets of His realm for mankind to reach for and promote a better world for all. This is the evolutionary process of mankind toward God's "unity with ultimate reality".

10

THE SALVATION OF HUMAN REASON IS ASSURED

The Reformation was a fractionalization of religion which gave a greater base for human interpretation and a more ego based earth bound religion.

Today, new churches arise while old churches disappear. Undoubtedly there is an evolution of churches taking place. This evolution is a product of new interpretations of scriptures, creating new churches with old fears based upon scriptures written from fear, persecution, persuasion and conversion.

Why should mankind fear its creator? Does one normally fear your mother or father? No, for they are a part of the process that gave you life.

Then why should you fear God, your ultimate Creator who gave you human reason, the divine nature toward virtue?

The newborn is the closest to God's purity in the lifespan of mankind. Maintaining the innocence and purity of a newborn is the greatest asset to the lifespan of a human being, for understanding your Creator's love is to understand your presence on earth has a destiny to serve your Creator's plans.

Fear is the incubator of hate and indifference, as fear is the opposite of love, for your presence on earth is the assurance of God's love or you would not be here.

Religion's emphasis on salvation creates a fear of enormous proportions and maintains a major portion of each religious doctrine.

This finds, in turn, much of each religious doctrine is composed of laws of moral and secular order. Secularism has been a major factor within religion's composition toward mankind's behavior.

Fear is the subsequent value that promotes the religious boundaries of mankind. God's boundaries of mankind are His gifts of human reason, **the divine nature God created within man toward virtue,** with a body composed of this earth. The gift of human reason is a small part of God Himself that will return to God upon death of the body which returns to earth. Mankind's salvation is assured because the Godly portion of mankind returns to God as the sensations of sin and human conquests return to earth.

The fear of salvation is a religious fallacy built upon a vision of body and soul being redeemed in total in heaven. The body of mankind is of this earth and never leaves this earth.

God is intellectual energy that perpetuates the evolutionary process of the universe. For man to conceptualize God in His true being is far beyond human reason.

The process of evolution in this world toward "unity with ultimate reality" is to gain a small fraction of the purity God offers in His grand plan throughout the universe. For mankind on this planet to understand they are only a minute part of God's universe is the beginning of understanding the purist and truest religion in which God's laws have nothing to do with the impurities created by man through fear, greed, wealth, power and above all, ego. **Thinking any human being is relative to God's intellectual energy is beyond mankind's spectrum of thought and knowledge.**

11

CENTURIES OF FEAR
WILL BE OVERCOME BY LOVE

Religion's mythical history stands in the way of religion's future. The emphasis on an Old Testament and New Testament are the writings and earthly assumptions of past authors for the basic contexts of most religions, which were written by the motivation of persuasion and conversion.

Abraham, Moses and the prophets dominate and create the context of Judaism, while Paul, Mark, Matthew and John dominate the context of Christianity.

Judaism brought to the world the monotheistic concept of one God. From Judaism's history both Islam and Christianity sprang forth with new contexts putting a visible face to God in Mohammad and Jesus.

Historically, fear and persecution have been a prominent factor of religious doctrine, making religion a state of laws and judgments, which in turn, has created greater fear and tumultuous fragmentation of religion.

The Reformation of the 1530's created a new religious world of past mythical history interpretation which created more fractions and less tolerance toward God's plan for mankind "unity with ultimate reality". The Reformation did nothing to correct the problems of religion, but only created more problematic indifferences that exist today which inhibit the world from understanding God's purpose for mankind's "unity with ultimate reality".

There is only one God; therefore there is only one religion, which is the desire of God for mankind's purpose on earth.

The evolutionary process of man on earth is to purify, not to pollute, not to consume—but to conserve. God did not create this world and the universe for one generation of mankind but for many generations of man to improve and bring a world and universe into a state of perpetual purity of soul and soil.

The current state of the world today, of consumption and religious indifferences, is leading mankind away from God's purpose for this world and for mankind.

Man must look to God's intellectual energy, which many call science to overcome the individual fear toward collection, which creates a contest of power, wealth, greed, murder, war and a possession of resources which limits distribution throughout the world.

God's religion is the purpose He perpetually creates man to purify and distribute the needed resources for each generation to continue the process of God's plan toward "unity with ultimate reality".

12

GOD IS THE PERFECTION OF INTELLECTUAL COMPASSION

Human reason is the divine nature God created within man toward virtue.

While man's body is composed of the earth, we can conclude the sensations, emotions, passions, stress, oppression and repressions come from the construct of our bodies made of this earth, therefore through sensation, emotion and passion comes sin. Consequently, we must conclude sin is of this earth.

Mankind's total context as a human being is both the divine nature of God, the virtue of human reason, and the body of sensations, emotions and passions therefore can conclude the basic conflict of mankind is between soul and body.

The purpose of purification is "unity with ultimate reality," is the purification of man's soul and also to ultimately purify the soil of the world to unify our souls with our bodies. This means today's pollution and consumption are contrary to God's purpose for man's destiny toward God's plan of "unity with ultimate reality".

God's religion is the unification toward purity of body and soul throughout the world and for all who populate his world.

Anselm, both a theologian and philosopher of meaning toward the doctrine of the first church brings to mind that "God is compassionate but not available to passion". Anselm's assumption presents a further fact of separation of human reason, being "the divine nature God created within man toward virtue and the body, composed of this earth, which presents the capability toward sensations and emotions that create passion". Compassion is of the virtue of human reason while passion is of the results created by sensations and emotions of the body. While compassion has the virtuous ability to understand, passion is the earthly force toward motivation and accomplishment. Passion has the complex ability to be both virtuous and sinful, based upon the needs to satisfy the needs of sensation and emotions that create passion.

Passion is of the sensations and emotions created by the body. Therefore the body is of this earth. Consequently, the earth is the factor toward both accomplishment and sins of this world, contrasting the divine nature God gave us toward virtue—human reason.

Frequently, passion overrules compassion in mankind's daily life as a visible reflection of assumed right of collection which includes power, wealth, greed, murder, corruption, war and in general, "the exclusion of many for the inclusion of a few".

Passion is a self-contained ambition toward satisfying a need of earthly dimension, while compassion is the concern outside one's self, which incorporates the virtue of human reason. "God, the ultimate magnitude of intellectual energy, the creator of space, time, matter and man has no body to create sensations, emotions and passion for God is not composed of this earth. God is the perfection of intellectual compassion, which assures all his creations their personal salvation within His realm of universal creation".

13

GOD'S VERB IS CAUSE

The divine nature God creates in man—human reason—is a part of God himself. Therefore the virtuous intellectual energy—the soul—returns to God upon the death of the body, which returns to earth for further purification. This is the salvation of mankind, *for man is God's tool to form matter for function while on this earth.*

Procreation is in itself forming of God's matter into another human being. **Mankind's daily efforts are the forming of matter into some useful purpose toward "unity with ultimate reality".**

While the earth is the substance of our bodies and our bodies are the subject of our sensations, emotion and passions, it is well to live within the realm of compassion while being motivated toward accomplishments by our passion. This is the will of God and should be mankind's objective of any and all endeavors.

The fractionalization and many varied interpretations of human manufactured literature considered sacred scriptures have created a great chasm toward God's plan of "unity with ultimate reality".

The Hebrew prophet Isaiah, chapter 29, verses 13 and 14, states "we are capable of hypocrisy for often we slip into routine forms of worship that mean nothing to us. If we want to be God's people we must be obedient and worship Him honestly and sincerely".

To worship God honestly and sincerely means no human intermediary concept or precept should proceed the thought of mankind between the creator and the creation.

Nature is God's will for His universe and all creations of His making. "Unity with ultimate reality" brings together the total will of God toward a universe of matter that is formed and purified toward perfection.

The ego of mankind has pointed to the purification of man toward salvation, while God's purpose is the purification of all his creations including the substance and composition of man; the earth.

God's verb is "cause". Within the spectrum of God's universe "cause" is the paramount reason for the existence of the universe, for without "cause" space, time, matter and energy would have no objective.

The mathematical progression of God's universe lies within the small becoming greater and the greater becoming small to becoming even greater. This is the universal process of birth and death throughout the universe. This is the universe "causality" of God's plan for "unity with ultimate reality".

Time presents change and change presents causes within the spectrum of space which give purpose to matter and ener-

gy that bring forth the celestial endeavors of the intellectual energy we call God, the Creator of time, space, matter
and energy.

Time is proof of God's relationship to a mathematical process of cause and effect, for the entire universe is a product of
mathematical causes and effects which mankind continues
to search for answers.

14

FAITH IS A PRODUCT OF HUMAN REASON

Human reason is the divine nature God has created within man toward virtue. Justice is the process of virtue, for justice must be served to obtain virtue.

Human reason is dependent upon knowledge which is gained through external perception. Consequently, quite often effects are better known than their cause. This is true with our knowledge of God. Nature—God's effect on mankind is better known than the cause of nature, God. Therefore if the effect—nature—exists, then the cause, God exists.

The effects of nature perceived through the external perception of mankind has created both religion and faith, which are metaphors supported by narratives limited by the author's location and environment.

Nature surrounds us each moment of our existence and through external perception of nature's effects, human reason begins to understand the priority of effects of nature and the cause—God—which in turn produces the metaphor—faith. *Faith is the product of human reason and God is the creator of human reason.*

Mankind's need to place the will of God, nature and nature's laws ahead of any and all religious doctrines throughout the world ahead of any precepts of the past is to promote the will of God ahead of what today's religious doctrines consider the will of God, based upon the past. God's interest is not mankind's past but mankind's future. A future that rids passion from mankind and replaces it with compassion, *a compassion that supplies the needs of existence throughout the world.*

Mankind through history changes with each generation, while man holds sacred the history of 4000 years ago. Placing faces of authority such as Abraham, Moses, Jesus, Mohammad and all the saints who appear more acquiescent of God's wishes than most, has diverted God's presence in our daily lives within the realm of His creation, nature.

To worship the past while living in the present is the conflict and confusion that exists today in religion. The world's prepondence of interpretation of the past, considered sacred, authored documents—authored out of different times and circumstances such as fear of persecution—should be considered reference, not sacred, for all were subject to different locations and environment.

Sacred should be the blessings God has given us, such as the world we live. Sacred should be the mandate to purify and not to pollute the soul nor the soil.

To purify God's creations is the reason and purpose God has created all creation for. The religion of the future will be the constant ambition to make better through purification of thoughts and deed which enhances the process of "unity with ultimate reality".

Mankind is more relevant to God when he looks to the future then the past. The future is what God wants us to do, while the past is what we have done. The essence of God is far beyond mankind's comprehension, consequently to assume God beyond the visible effects of nature is a presumption of unassured consequences, which permeates many religious doctrines today.

15

WHEN CHANGE IS ACCEPTED, THE PAST WILL NO LONGER DETERMINE THE FUTURE

Mankind's concept of "first causes" refers to the laws of nature and the first priority of God's laws. Causability is God's intellectual energy that creates effects that create other causability and effects that create further causability. This is the evolvement of change which is the evolutionary force toward "unity with ultimate reality".

Foremost, causability is the prime effect God performs for creation. Change is constant, therefore God's evolutionary process is constant. The lifespan of mankind represents change, such as birth to death. St. Augustine said, "I die a little each day".

Mankind's ability toward change is limited by lack of vision and complacency. The comfort of the present is preferred over the uncertainty of the future. While this is the limitation of human existence, God's plan of "unity with ultimate reality" continues evolving.

The history of time points out God, the creator of biological evolution, is then followed by mankind's cultural evolution which creates the identity for each generation of mankind. This again is a product of location and environment by geological consent.

The generational culture of "unity with ultimate reality" will have the identity of each human being on earth released from the bondage of spending time and space for the necessities of existence and the misery of need.

God's rule over space and time are absolute, but his tools of the formation of matter, man and mankind's human reason provide earthly limitations because of a reluctance toward change.

Mankind's history of reluctance toward change has somewhat changed with the widespread distributions of computers. The evolutionary force of future computerization present greater change than most human minds can comprehend. Therefore knowledge, "the ability toward recollection," will allow greater speed of change while mankind will struggle to maintain reference to the available knowledge and its use. The computer age and the next generation of knowledge retrieval will prompt questions of causability and effects throughout the universe.

God's will and destiny for man will become more clairvoyant but limited by the educational level of the populace. Education and government possess limiting powers toward change. Government of the future will have to discard industrial profit for citizen welfare. The countries of the world are limited in progress by the poverty that exists within their populace. Profit must submit to poverty to meet the educational needs of a better world of understanding and growth toward "unity with ultimate reality".

The current condition of fractionalization of the world today in government, religion and ideologies is limiting the process of mankind toward "unity with ultimate reality".

The inability to know and understand the desires and needs of people have created limited progression toward a world of understanding and progress toward "unity with ultimate reality".

While the world is interested in production, distribution appears to have little importance. The concept of profit through production appears to be considerably greater than distribution toward mankind's needs and desires which create greater customer bases for industry.

To predict the timetable toward "unity with ultimate reality" will take considerable changes in mankind's concepts toward humanity and the reason for being. Many generations have passed between now and the Neanderthals, who lived between 130,000 BC and 30,000 BC. Consequently, present day concepts of myth constructing history and the many powers of collection inhibit a troubled mind of secular nature from a mind of compassion and generosity with "unity with ultimate reality".

Mankind's reliance upon a superficial past promoting laws of social and moral order based upon fear will be replaced by the natural order of God's creation, nature. While man cannot circumvent God's laws of nature, the presumption of past sacred events based upon fear, anxiety and oppression will not serve mankind in the future toward the ultimate purpose of God's creation "unity with ultimate reality," God and His ultimate world for man.

16

UNIVERSAL REASON IS GOD'S GIFT TO HUMANITY TOWARD VIRTUE

Mankind's freedom of thought has been impaired by the turning inward by institutional revelation as a source of knowledge.

Judaism, Christianity and Islam are religions of laws built upon the fears of past revelation and denying the freedom of God's nature as presented to mankind each and every day. The created fears of past revelations create more passions than compassions. Passions have created significant reasons of misunderstanding which have lead to a history of wars and slaughter of God's creations.

Mankind's soul is the manifestations of universal reason which is God's gift to mankind. Universal reason toward virtue is the true desire of God's purpose for mankind.

God's nature is the design of the true religion God has placed before mankind to follow as a religion. This departs from all destruction of God's creations which forbids war and conflict and places a higher degree toward reason and understanding than mankind has practiced in the past. The wars and conflicts and the magnitude of destruction of God's creations proves mankind is still in a state of barbaric emotions and passions of collection.

A state of human bondage occurs when reason is replaced by confused, fragmentary ideas thrust on people who then become sporadic, inordinate, unpredictable and obsessive. This creates panic, jealousy and overmastering loves and hates. These passions and emotions are all origins of fear. When mankind replaces these origins of fear with reason, a distinctive form of joy occurs within mankind. For knowledge has replaced fear and mankind has a sense of freedom toward obtainment of the next level of reason.

"Unity with ultimate reality" is the obtainment of the levels of reason placed before mankind toward purity of soul and soil. **This is the purpose God places on mankind to elevate a world of virtue through reason toward the intellectual energy, God.**

Today, the world's religions have created an indifferent and complex myriad of doctrines and laws that have polarized the world's population into fragmented groups of ego inspired righteousness that are far from God's obvious laws toward mankind, nature.

God speaks to mankind through his creations of universality. This means there is only one God and one religion. Mankind's ability to interpret and understand God's nature brings together a world of understanding of God's purpose for mankind.

Judaism, Christianity and Islam are institutionalizations of turning inward toward a personal salvation and purity of soul. Purity of soul is guaranteed for mankind's soul is the gift of God at birth for human reason is the divine nature God created within man toward virtue. The gift of human reason returns to God after the death of the body which returns to the earth's soil.

Human reason, the gift of God's virtue is only on loan while the body occupies space on earth.

17

WHEN THE NECESSITIES OF LIFE ARE ASSURED TO ALL THEN WE WILL KNOW THE COMPASSION OF GOD

For mankind to reach "unity with ultimate reality" today's concepts of good government and right religion will drastically change.

Today, democracy is believed to be the ultimate individual freedom while totally dependent upon capitalism. Capitalism's ultimate path of progress is oligarchy and eventual monopoly. Both oligarchy and monopoly are functions that deprive individual freedom by limiting access of resources to many while rewarding a few.

God's plan of "unity with ultimate reality" does not put the power of resources in a certain few but to allow all His creations their systemic ability to perform a unity of perfection which becomes God's world of "unity with ultimate reality". Good government of the future will be distribution of resources to all to realize the full potential of God's creations.

The current deprivation of resources to the body's needs throughout the world limits the universal will of progress to all mankind. The will and ambition of power and profit succeeds to the disposition of fear and hunger. When the people of this world no longer have a fear of the supply of bodily needs, the minds of the world will begin to fulfill the purpose God created mankind for. This will begin an era of knowledge not yet known to mankind.

When wealth succumbs to knowledge, mankind will begin to understand God's purpose for his creation. When government succeeds from wealth and profit to distribution, religion which has been promoted by secular wealth and myth must return to a time in history where myth did not create history.

The present day finds technology in advance of humanity. To obtain "unity with ultimate reality" it appears the possibility technology will create greater awareness and importance of humanity. This will require a knowledge of pride over profit.

The change in governments and religions throughout the world toward a concept of "unity with ultimate reality" seems quite remote with the many fragmentations of both governments and religions. But God's manifestations of nature points to the ultimate destiny of mankind.

Mankind cannot escape from God's purpose of his creation of mankind. While governments squander humanity through poverty and mismanagement, religion purports its many fragmentations of faith based upon history that has been based upon myth and oracles. Meanwhile, the essence of God, nature, is both ignored and taken for granted. Mankind's reliance to the future is through the eyes of nature which exposes itself each moment, each day, each year to all mankind. Nature and its blessings are the greatest gifts from God to man.

Through a religion based upon the realities of nature, which we know for certain is the work of our Creator, mankind can obtain both purity of soul and soil and find "unity with ultimate reality".

18

FOSSIL CONVENTIONALISM

Religion is a human endeavor principally based upon the fear of retribution of the afterlife.

The fear of retribution has created believing as an act of volition, meaning one comes to believe something because one wills to believe it. Since fear of retribution is a learned fear, the metaphors of religion have corrupted God's assurance of safe passage of the soul back to God.

With the emphasis on the past sacred literary teachings of laws of obedience, religion today is relying upon "fossil conventionalism." "Fossil conventionalism" is the attempt to justify religion by pointing to its privileged origin in some kind of previous revelation. Presently, religion is running a gauntlet of confrontation based upon its reliance of the past.

God's "unity with ultimate reality" will lift mankind's mindset to a new enlarged knowledge capacity and allow naturalism to exist toward a peaceful co-existence of maintenance toward a better world of future generations.

"Unity with ultimate reality" is the object of God's knowledge as an ideal world order, which decidedly differs from the real world order insofar as the latter is in some form measured in accord with man's limited freewill.

Through an act of God's will, God created the world in time and space and imposed on it the order of nature. The order of nature is God's laws and the truest of religions by God.

Knowledge is the sum of collection. Consequently, the collection ability of the computer and the computer age has increased the speed of evolution toward a new high in human development.

At this time with technology in advance of humanity there appears to be a possible evolutionary breakthrough toward a psychic evolution and the development of new concepts of man and spirit.

The psychic evolution has put into question the 2000-year-old Jesus story. While the gospel narratives have been simplified and domesticated for children and adults alike, subservience has been the desired outcome and in many cases achieved.

The psychic evolution has put into question the validity of the biblical literature of the first 2000 years AD. The placement of Jesus before and equal to God has become increasingly dysfunctional.

The priority of Jesus before God prompts a human image of earth bound nature that appears to satisfy the ego of mankind while the magnificence of God and God's work of evolutionary nature continues to be denied by the story of creation.

The perseverance of the sacredness of the bible has impeded the future of religion. Mankind's insistence of his personal worth toward God's purpose for the world has superseded the worth of mankind over the worth of the world. Mankind's purpose is to be God's caretaker toward an eventual world of external justice as mankind will continue to serve God through predestination of God's purpose with human reason and limited freewill.

The nature of the world will replace the past sacred scripture and reality will replace fantasy. This will bring mankind closer to God's purpose for His creation.

19

GOD WILL WIN

God's plan of mathematical cyclical nature termed **evolution** has an exponent of acceleration, which has been decidedly accelerated by the advent of the computer age. The intellect of mankind is enhanced by the ability to collect knowledge. The computer's ability to collect knowledge has put mankind into an increasingly accelerated rate of intellectual endeavor.

To define "mathematical cyclical nature" is to recognize how the association of elementary particles constitute atoms, atoms constitute molecules, and molecules constitute even larger organisms which represent the progressive development of order from the initial chaos of nature. Order means a mathematical progression. *A form of order is sought by all living things.*

Mankind is subject to cultural heritage more than genetic heritage. This means, unlike the apian society of the bees, the maintenance of self-preservation is within the genetic structure whereas the human must be taught and does not have automatic transmittal through the physical process of generation.

Teaching is the paramount instrument of the order and progression of mankind toward "unity with ultimate reality."

A world where the formation of matter is optimized and the welfare of mankind is so ordered with God and God's purpose that transgressions are scarce within the order of society.

The Apian society, the bees who rely upon the genetic heritage for automatic transmittal of the physical process of re-generation, is another example of God's determinism, whereas mankind's forming of matter such as art, sculpture, a bridge, a building, a nation, a country is an example of mankind's free will limited by God's determinism of location and environment.

"Unity with ultimate reality" is when mankind of this world accepts the legitimacy of "God's cosmic justice of virtue" as the ultimate rule for all mankind. Within the hearts and beliefs of mankind, the truth and value of God's cosmic justice is not yet known.

Religion and society's free will has created chaotic versions of righteousness that have only created greater indifferences which hopefully within the future of intellectual integrity will find the true will of God and turn toward "unity with ultimate reality."

With the current indifferences of society and religion throughout the world, to mankind it appears impossible to see one world in agreement. But since there is only one God, one true religion of God's making, nature, mankind will ultimately realize the human emotions of greed, anger, hate promote indifference that disallow the social stability and happiness of "unity with ultimate reality" through the "virtue of cosmic justice".

To say mankind today is a long way from "unity with ultimate reality" is an understatement, but God's determinism for His will and desires for his world is a far greater force than the limited free will He has bestowed upon mankind.

"Unity with ultimate reality", is God's desire for this world through His gift of human reason to mankind which ultimately submits to the determinism of God.

CHAPTER ONE

20

A SUMMARY
TOWARD LIFE IN THE FUTURE

The meaning of life lies within the purpose of life, which is God's creation of mankind to form matter for function. Procreation is the priority toward continued generational process of forming matter throughout the universe.

The meaning of life for each human being lies within the perceptions of location and environment. Human existence does not escape the determinants of location and environment.

Time is relevant to location and environment and creates change, for without time there is no change, for the nature of time is change. God created time to create change toward the evolutionary process "unity with ultimate reality."

Time is relevant to God's cosmic justice, which finds no rationality in unfulfilled human needs of necessity within today's world. A democracy of capitalism based upon power and greed has replaced the author's intent, Adam Smith's capitalism of sympathy and empathy.

The imposed determinants created by greed and power compromise location and environment and limit freewill and achievement for those subject to the poverty created by power and greed.

When mankind achieves the age of "unity with ultimate reality" ethics will be the first philosophy of the human leadership which will find an order of government that will provide the basic needs of human necessity throughout the world.

Future world leadership will take away the will to dominate humanity from the power of poverty toward basic human needs.

The age of "unity with ultimate reality" will recognize the importance of basic human care for the populace of the world which will eliminate the anxieties and animosities of basic needs. The will of power will be narrowed to the ideologies and doctrines of the just and unjust. This will call into question the identities of the various doctrines of all scriptural monotheism.

Presently a sharp contrast of religious doctrine is in a state of conflict and debate. The past history of the Judeo-Christian religion has been based upon a drama of tragedy and hope for a future life of a higher order, while today's materialistic world has created a persona of self assurance toward citizenship justice that has evolved into a civic religion of secular humanism.

Mankind is yet to realize human reason is a very small portion of the intellectual energy of God and returns to God after the body dies and returns to earth.

Within the spectrum of God's universal knowledge, mankind lives in a poverty stricken world, for it's quite possible death of the body reveals to the soul (human reason) the poverty of knowledge of this world and allows soul (human reason) the privilege of experiencing the unlimited universal knowledge of God, the Creator.

Death of the body relieves the limitations of knowledge of limited location and environment and human reason (soul) as captive to the body's needs for existence. Human reason (soul) is only subject then to the universal needs of God, the Creator.

The earthbound limitations of freedom are many such as secular laws and the metaphors created by Judaism, Christianity and Islam, for God makes no promises except life itself.

To understand the metaphoric atmosphere of Judaism is to examine the book of Genesis, which was written and authored from about 900 BC to 584 BC. This was about the time the Jewish people were exiled from Babylon.

Genesis tells us of the willingness of Abraham to sacrifice son Isaac through his fear of God. This metaphor of the willingness toward God's creations, created by the fear of the mystery of the relationship between life and death is a total misunderstanding of God's purpose for the creation of mankind. **The purpose for mankind is to form matter for function, not to destroy the matter God created.**

Judaism's narrative changed dramatically when in 60 AD, Judaism's second temple was destroyed by the Romans, which left no place for sacrifice. Judaism's narrative became today's rabbinic doctrine and teaching.

Christianity's Saul of Tasus, alias Paul was the provider of the universality of Christianity. Paul's churches and teaching brought a remote Jewish figure into an icon of universal appeal.

Again, like Judaism, Christianity became a metaphor of the drama of tragedy built upon the sacrifices of God's creations to seek martyrdom. Christianity's metaphor is based upon the sacrifice of Jesus, Abraham, James, Jesus' brother, Paul and the disciples of Jesus.

Christianity's narrative is attempting to find favor with God while sacrifices, war and killing are diametrically opposed to God's will for mankind to form matter toward function.

God's purpose of harmony throughout the world toward "unity with ultimate reality" is pre-empted and delayed by wars—slaughter of God's creations which all have purpose—while killing all of which shortens the life span of the purpose. The narrative of Christianity's drama of tragedy is under scrutiny and dramatic changes will come in future Christian narratives.

The narrative of Islam has many secular interpretations, which have promoted confusion and violence. The willingness of killing as the alternative to conversion is totally out of context with God's will for universal harmony toward "unity with ultimate reality."

God's will for mankind is orthopraxy (right living) and orthodoxy (right thinking) which cannot be forced or coerced upon the human being. The basic content of right living and right thinking is freedom, the God given ability toward choices. Freedom toward choices allows a vision of the universal will of God toward "unity with ultimate reality." The many restrictions imposed by the doctrines and laws of Judaism, Christianity and Islam promote the past and restrict the future.

Mankind's ego and self worth, combined with the fear of death has created religious narratives that are earth bound. The concept of freedom, within the context of Genesis, assumes a personal relationship between God and mankind that assumes a degree of equality. Nothing could be farther from the truth, for mankind is subject to the limitations of location and environment, while God is not. **God's perspective is the universe** while mankind's perspective is a very limited area on earth with the influence of very limited knowledge of that particular space, time and the matter available at that time and space.

The narratives that have created the metaphors of religion today are weak and being resisted by God's truth of harmony toward "unity with ultimate reality." God's purpose of "unity with ultimate reality" cannot be denied and the virtue of God's gift of human reason to mankind will, through the generalization process of mankind on earth, obtain the harmony of "unity with ultimate reality." This will incorporate a new religious narrative of unification that will provide care and comfort to all mankind through the will of God and the nature of God. This will replace the many current concepts of mankind's self worth and salvation built upon oracles and myths that have become scripture through fear, based upon limited location and environment of the past.

As promised within the first chapter of this book I have attempted to put a face on the meaning of life, the importance of freedom, the quality of life and the relevance of life to death. The future will assume the importance of these four questions over the dominance of power and profit for God's will of "unity with ultimate reality" will become reality.

·